# THE
## *Old Man's Guide*
### TO *Health &*
## *Longer Life*

# THE
# *Old Man's Guide*
## TO *Health & Longer Life*

WITH *Rules* FOR
*Diet, Exercise & Physick*
FOR
*Preserving* A *Good Constitution*,
AND *Preventing Disorders*
IN A *Bad One*

JOHN HILL

THE BRITISH LIBRARY

This edition published in 2013 by
The British Library
96 Euston Road
London NW1 2DB

First published in 1750

British Library Cataloguing-in-Publication Data
A catalogue record for this book is available from The British Library

ISBN 978 0 7123 5898 9

Designed and typeset in Monotype Jansen by illuminati, Grosmont
Cover designed by Lucy Morton at illuminati
Printed in Hong Kong by Great Wall Printing Co. Ltd

PICTURE CREDITS   British Library: 13 7744.c.10; 21, 41, 59 c.58.cc.1.(2);
23 7031.v.4; 24 1509/4460; 29 Maps K.Top.xxix.7-q; ii, 38, 64, 70 1267.f.15;
47 12330.m.28. British Museum: 6, 14, 33, 42, 55, 62, 68.

# Contents

# To the reader

HEALTHFUL OLD AGE is the most valuable and happy period of human life. Experience has render'd the ancient more able than those who have seen less, and felt less, to conduct themselves and their descendants; and being freed from the empire of the passions, they enjoy quiet.

Philosophy pretends to this condition, but age gives it truly. Whatever their heirs may think, it is worth preserving, and in that sense I write the present Treatise. A hundred are cut off at this advanced period by disorders which a proper regimen might have prevented, for every one who dies of age, or its unavoidable effects. Many fall by accidents, to one who is fairly call'd away by nature: and these accidents and disorders it is proposed here to give the means of avoiding.

Old men's diseases are hard to cure, but they are easily prevented: and the same means which preserve their health give happiness. It must be a good natural fabrick which has preserved itself entire so long, and thro' so many chances; and the same strength will keep it, perhaps, much longer together under a good regulation. Moderate diet and proper exercise are the best guardians of the health of old and young, and in the advanced period here considered there are two great preservatives besides. These are ease of mind and cheerfulness of disposition. Both are the natural offspring of health; and they will continue the blessing to which they owe their origin.

We shall consider first the hale and healthy old man; and afterwards the weakly, and the sick. For our purpose is first to direct those how to preserve health who have it, and afterwards to restore or to recover it where it is attack'd or enfeebled by diseases.

# CHAPTER I

## *How the old man may know he is in health*

'TIS ALLOW'D that we know so little of nothing, as of ourselves. This has been said principally of the mind, but it is scarce less true of the body. The fancying we have diseases will often bring them upon us; and there is as much danger in forcing ourselves to believe against our feeling that we are well, when some disorder is in the body. This is the less common error, but there are more instances of it than may be thought.

To avoid both let the old man read here with a free mind. Let him not suppose, because God has blessed him with long health, he is above the reach of sickness; nor neglect the care which may conquer, in its beginning, a disease that will else in the end conquer him. Let him be as ready to acknowledge real disorders, as careful to avoid the imaginary.

Health consists in a good digestion of the food, and a free circulation of the blood. The appetite and the condition of the stomach after eating will shew the first; and the latter may be known best by the pulse.

That old person's digestion is good, who has a sharp but not voracious appetite; and who feels no pain or sickness after meals. To preserve this let him always be content with less than the full of what he could eat: for the sure way to keep the stomach in order is not to overload it.

The time of feeling the pulse is in the morning, some time after getting up, and before breakfast. It should be a rule never to omit this examination. A constant and regular attention to it will shew the slighest variations; and whenever such happen, care must be taken of the health.

There are mechanical methods of counting the strokes by a watch, but the plainer way is better. The general regular measure is seventy-four strokes in a minute, but pulses differ greatly in various persons; and nature may be injur'd by forcing her toward a condition she, perhaps, never had, nor requires.

A frequent examination will inform any person what is the condition of the pulse when in health; and the deviations from this are the rules to know sickness.

While an old man feels his pulse regular, finds his digestion good, and with a mind at ease can take his usual exercise freely, he may laugh at the expectation of the next in inheritance. He may be certain he is well; and we shall tell him how to keep so. For when the fault is seen in time it is easily remedy'd. If the pulse beat too quick and high the diet must be a little lower; if too slow, and weak, the food must be richer. This short direction will prevent diseases.

The doctors will not thank me for this, but I do not write it for their service: they must own 'tis true, tho' they dislike the publishing of it. If men would pay more regard to their own constitutions, they would want little of their assistance; which always comes too late to prevent mischief, and often to relieve it.

# CHAPTER II

# *Of preserving a healthful state in old age*

EXERCISE HAS thro' the younger part of life been very instrumental in preserving the health. When we grow old we cannot use so much; and we must therefore be doubly careful in our diet. That will go off with exercise, which will overload the body when kept quiet: that will nourish while we walk abroad, which, when we stay at home, breeds fevers. The less exercise we use the less we should eat; and what we do eat should be of the milder nature.

We must not make this change violently: for all sudden alterations in the diet are dangerous. Our strength for exercise will leave us by degrees, and we must reduce our food in quantity and quality accordingly; by a little at a time, not by a harsh change at once.

Winter is the season when old men are least healthy; therefore they must then be most careful. They are colder than young persons, therefore cold more affects them. The weakness of their circulation makes them cold, and this is known by their feeble and slow pulse. They will know therefore that the cold weather has hurt them, when they perceive the pulse more weak and slow than usual. They must preserve themselves against it; and recover the new damage by more warmth, and a somewhat higher diet.

If perspiration have been stop'd by external cold, and no other ill effect follow, it will be seen by the urine being paler and more in quantity than usual. In this case let flannel be put on carefully. It will encrease, or restore the perspiration, and the urine will come to its due colour and quantity: after that let it be very carefully left off again.

The good we shew it can do, proves it may also do harm. Health consists in the evacuations having all their proper course and quantity; and flannel will diminish one as much as it encreases another. No disorder is more troublesome to old people than costiveness: and the use of flannel improperly will sometimes occasion this, by taking off too much of the natural moisture.

By this, as by the other rules, the old person will see that a careful attention to his health is the only way to preserve it: and that things are excellent when properly used, which may otherwise be destructive. If the appetite fail, or wind oppress the stomach after meals, let the person take more air and exercise, and read or study less: for much study always hurts the digestion; and when that is impaired, worse mischiefs will follow.

# CHAPTER III

# *Of the diet of old men*

It has been customary to recommend a particular diet to old persons, as if one course of living could suit all constitutions: but this is very wrong. Old men differ as much from one another, as old from young; and according to their several constitutions, a various course of life is necessary in this respect. Therefore we shall establish no peculiar diet as fit for every old person, but only lay down certain general rules. These will hold universally, because they are calculated for old people, merely as they are old; not as they are of one or another constitution.

Lighter diet is more proper for aged persons than young; and this in their liquors as well as solid food.

Beef and pork should be avoided: for the stomach will rarely be able to digest these when it is not assisted by exercise.

Lamb, veal, pig, chickens, and tame rabbet are very excellent food for old persons; and out of these, if there are no others, a tolerable management may produce sufficient variety.

No aged person should eat more than one meal of solid food in the day. The stomach will be able to manage a dinner when the breakfast and supper have been light: otherwise the load of one meal not being gone off before another is brought in, neither will be digested.

The substantial meal should be dinner; and this should not be eaten too early, that the appetite may not be violent for supper. It has been observed already, that the quantity of food at a meal should be less for old persons than for young: and the older they grow, the more this should be diminished. This was the practice of Hippocrates; and by the observance of it Carnaro lived to his extreme age.

This regulation principally concerns dinner, which is the capital meal. With respect to supper, the lighter it is the better; though we do not agree with those who advise the omitting that meal intirely. Moderation is the rule of health in all life, but most of all in the old man's life. They were in the right who declared the mischief of solid or heavy suppers, but the poets have long since said what sort of people those are, who, in avoiding a fault, rush into its contrary. There is a medium between a heavy supper and emptiness; and this is best. Since all agree solid food at this meal is wrong, let the old man eat liquid; and of all liquid diets, those which are partly composed of milk are best.

'Tis only in the extreme of age that men become children again in their understandings. Yet in their bodily faculties they approach this condition sooner: for they grow weak as they grow aged, and weakness is weakness whether it be in old men or children. For this reason the food of children is fit for them, at least in the lesser meal. Their digestive faculties are less powerful, but milk is in a manner ready digested. They want an easy nourishment; and this affords it, without loading the stomach, or oppressing it during the hours of rest.

Asses milk is most easy of digestion, and most nourishing; and a pint of that, with a small toast,

eaten two hours before bedtime, will be nourishing, and sit easy on the stomach. The value of asses milk is its lightness: that of the cow is richer and heavier. Those who use the latter in this case in the country should mix it first with equal parts of soft water: in London this care is unnecessary, as those who sell milk do it for them.

There are many other methods in which milk is pleasant and proper: milk pottage, thin rice milk, and other such dishes, will give a variety without having recourse to other things. But some farther change is not denied them: weak broths of veal, chicken, and mutton may be eaten occasionally, and jellies honestly made at home are proper, safe, and nourishing.

With this choice, the old man need not desire meat suppers; and these things will answer the double purpose of nourishing and moistening the body; for aged persons are naturally too dry in their constitutions.

The breakfast is the only meal remaining to be considered, and this is not a very important one. Those who eat no supper are too hungry in the morning; and the stomach is loaded with what they take at that time, and therefore is the less able to digest a dinner.

This is the reason we advise old persons to eat suppers, provided they be of a right kind. These take the edge off the morning's appetite, and there will remain just so much desire to eat as will lead them to get something into the stomach without loading it.

This is necessary to health. We know men may fast away their appetite; and their power of digestion goes in a great measure with it. The conduct of the appetite regulates the health; and this is not enough regarded. Young people may take liberties with themselves, for nature is strong: but the older must pay more regard to her weakness.

It is as essential to health not to keep the stomach empty, as not to overload it. Wind is the consequence of emptyness, and this disturbs the office of the stomach. It should be always kept at its due employment in advanced periods of life; and this by small quantities of proper food.

For these plain reasons, breakfasts are as proper, nay as necessary, as suppers. Those who are troubled with phlegm should eat less at this meal than others, but all should eat some. A cup of chocolate, not made too strong, is a good breakfast. Coffee I cannot advise generally: but the exceptions against tea are in a great measure groundless.

Those who drink a great quantity of tea, and are careless in the making of it, using a bad kind, and drinking the last dishes cool and palled, will unquestionably weaken their stomachs: but this is not the case with such as are more careful. If the old man likes tea he need not deny it to himself for breakfast. Let him use the plain green tea, of sixteen shillings a pound, and make it well: taking care the water boils, and allowing so much tea that it may be of sufficient strength without standing too long upon the leaves. This way we have the spirit, flavour, and virtue of the plant; whereas weak, half cold, bad tea has just the contrary qualities.

Let the old man drink three moderate cups of this tea, with a little sugar and a good deal of milk; and swallow it neither too hot, nor mawk-ishly cool. Let him eat with it a thin slice or two of good bread, with a little butter; and he will find it nourishing and excellent.

The virtues of tea thus drank are as considerable as its bad qualities when ill managed. In this manner, it strengthens the stomach, and assists digestion. It keeps the body from being empty without loading it; and the appetite for dinner will be the better, and the digestion also more perfect. To this we are to add, that tea in this quantity is sufficient for the great purpose of diluting; and that it refreshes the spirits more than any other liquid.

The best drink at meals is malt liquor, not too strong, and neither new nor stale. For this reason small ale is better than table-beer, because it will bear keeping to a due time for safe use. For the more cordial liquors, wine is the best. A little of this is necessary to old men, and according to the constitution and former manner of life, more may be borne without inconvenience, or indeed with advantage. The kind of wine must be suited to the peculiarity of the constitution, of which we shall treat hereafter: here we speak generally. But for most old persons, of all wines sack is the best, if it can be obtained pure and genuine.

As occasion shall require the supper foods here directed may be used by way of dinner; and broths may be necessary some times for breakfast. This will be known from the circumstances. When the stomach cannot digest solids, these liquid nourishments must supply the place; and when more nourishing things are wanted, a broth breakfast is excellent. Vipers are extolled, but 'tis an idle fancy: I have found, on repeated tryals, broth of veal and chickens is better.

# CHAPTER IV

## Of the foods old men should avoid

After directing what is proper, we shall conclude this article of diet, by pointing out those things which are hurtful to persons advanced in years: and this is the more necessary because many of them are unsuspected.

Every thing that is heavy, and hard of digestion, must be avoided: and tho' vegetables may be thought innocent, there are many cases in which they prove hurtful.

No general praise, or general censure, can be passed upon them in this respect; for they differ according to their kinds as much as animal foods.

Carrots are to be avoided, for no old stomach can digest them. On the contrary potatoes are innocent, and parsnips are nourishing.

Among herbage raw sallads should be shunned. Cabbage, and all its kinds, breed wind, and are therefore wrong: but asparagus is diuretick; and is excellent against that common old man's complaint, the gravel.

Heavy cheese should be carefully avoided; and there is nothing worse than eating too much butter: but very fine Cheshire cheese, or the parmezan in a small quantity after other food, are not amiss.

All sharp tasted things, whether food or drink, are carefully to be shunned. They cannot be neutral upon the stomach; and they are much more likely to do harm than good. Such things are to be considered as medicines, and as carefully used.

Fruits in general are to be avoided by old men; but of all others, most carefully raw pears.

Wall-fruit, and the other produce of our garden trees and shrubs, when they have grown in a good soil, and are exactly of a due degree of ripeness, are innocent. Yet this is the best that can be said of them, and to deserve this all those circumstances are requisite; otherwise they hurt the stomach and often bring on cholicks.

Cucumbers, and the like productions of the kitchen garden, weaken the digestion, and greatly prevent the natural and necessary secretions.

The pine-apple, the most pleasant of all fruit, is the most dangerous. Its sharpness flays the mouth; and 'tis easy to know what effect such a thing must have upon the stomach and bowels of persons weakened by age. I have known it bring on bloody fluxes, which have been fatal. There are several kinds of this fruit somewhat differing in quality, and the perfect degree of ripeness in

a great measure takes off its bad effects. Yet these are nice distinctions; and he who is wise will judge as he does of mushrooms: where many are dangerous, avoid all.

Beside avoiding things which are hurtful in themselves, those who are far advanced in years should be upon their guard against such as they are not accustom'd to. Particular constitutions, in medicine, will shew unforeseen aversions to particular things: and it is the same in foods. Let him who knows what agrees with him stick to that. Change is wrong, and it may be hazardous: and 'tis idle to run into the way of danger when there is no advantage.

All mixtures of food upon the stomach are bad; and there is not a greater error in an old person than to eat of many things at one meal. He must not deceive himself by arguing that all are innocent: two things of known qualities will often on the mixing produce a third that is perfectly different from them both; and these are dangerous trials in an old man's stomach. The management in these articles is nearly as important as the choice; and a regularity of eating is the next care to the selecting proper food, and fixing on a right quantity.

# CHAPTER V

## *Of air for old persons*

NOTHING CONTRIBUTES more to health and long life than pure and good air: but by pure we are not to understand bleak; nor are old men at any time to chuse it. It is strange, that many live to a great age in London, where the air has neither of these characters: where we breathe smoak, and the mixt stench of a thousand putrifying substances, which cannot evaporate through the thick and foul atmosphere of the place.

But though none will question the superior quality of a clear country air, yet let not him who has attained to a healthy threescore and ten then think of leaving London, to continue his days to a longer period. They say use is a second nature. It becomes nature itself; and bad things, to which an old man has been very long accustomed, are better than sudden changes. It is well known, some who have reached an uncommon date of life, have perished at last by a sudden change in their food; and the air is scarce of less consequence.

He who would increase the period, and the healthy condition of his days by a country air, should begin it at an earlier time, when his constitution can better bear the shock of alteration.

In regard to choice of air, the reason we declare against that which is too bleak is plain, for bleak and cold are always found together. Cold air chills the blood, and in old men we want rather to warm it. This is the air at the tops of hills: and such situations all old men should avoid.

On the contrary, the warmest air of the country is that of vallies, sheltered by rising grounds: but this is usually damp; and more mischief will arise from it than good.

Therefore the choice rests solely upon a gentle ascent. The best place of all is toward the bottom of a ground, which does not in any part rise to a very great height; and if there be a running water at the bottom it is so far perfect.

But more than this must be consulted for the country residence of the old man, or of any who would live to be old. The soil is of vast consequence; and so is the exposure. A clayey bottom must be avoided; because it is always cold, and the air about it raw and damp. Rains cannot get thro' it, and they lodge till they are evaporated, chilling the ground, and loading the air with their moisture.

A clean gravel is the best of all. The air over this is warm, and naturally dry; for rain soaks through it.

The north and north-east winds are worst for old men: therefore let them shelter themselves from these by a proper choice of situation. Let the descent of the ground face the south-west; and then the natural rise will keep off the bleak and cold air from the opposite quarters. This may be assisted by plantations of trees; and thus the true feat of health and pleasure may be established, so far as these great points concern them.

He is happy who has made such a choice in time; and he still happier who finds himself now in good time to make it. The later such a residence is chosen, the more carefully must the owner accustom himself to it: first in summer; and by

degrees and at times at other periods of the year. An air thus chosen, will then give all the great articles age wants, appetite, digestion, and a free circulation.

Exercise will be easy; and it will be pleasant in such a spot: but let this be under the regulation of good sense. Nothing is better than walking; but let not the old man do himself more hurt by a rash and careless indulgence in this than it can do him service. Let him never enjoy the air but when it is in a condition to do him good; nor venture upon the ground but when it is fit for his feet.

No country house is without a garden; and the best part of this will be a good gravel walk. Let it be open to the south-west, and well defended from the dangerous quarters. Let it be laid tolerably round, that the water may not lodge; and let it be kept well rolled, hard and smooth.

In favourable weather he may walk in pathways in the fields: but in such as is not so good, this walk will be highly useful. Let him never come upon it till the dew is off the grass; and let the setting sun be the last object he sees from it; even in the best weather.

The air of early morning and of late evening is cold and unwholesome: but some hours of the first part of the day passed constantly on such a walk will add many years to life; and what is much better, it will give health with them.

# CHAPTER VI

## *Of exercise for old men*

AIR LED US to mention already the first of exercises, which is walking; and for those who can indulge themselves in this, there is none better: but feebleness and various accidents often deny its use to those who most of all want motion. In this case, riding on horseback is the next in excellence. And the best hours of the day must be chosen for that, in the same manner as for the other. In severe weather it is necessary to keep under shelter; and at all times to avoid damp or bleak places.

Diversions afford excellent exercise. Bowling is one: but the same care must be taken, that this be at a proper time. A chariot may supply the place of a horse to those who are more feeble; and when even this is too much, there will be a great deal of good in being driven along in those chairs which are made to run about garden-walks.

To those who are fond of gardening, nothing affords so happy, or so constant exercise. We do not mean that they should dig, or weed the ground, but that employment which will give exercise without labour, and which no hand will so well perform as that of the Master: the trimming of shrubs, and flowering plants, the management of espaliers; the removal of seedling-flowers; the thinning of fruit upon the trees; and the following and overlooking of several other works. Here will at least be more and more brisk walking than otherwise; and in many things the little use of the hands will compleat that exercise, continuing it perfectly through the body.

The only danger of this healthy and happy course, is that it is too tempting. Let him who falls into it take an invariable resolution, never to let his fondness for the garden carry him out too early, or keep him out too late.

# CHAPTER VII

## *Of substitutes for exercise*

THE BENEFIT of exercise all know; but all cannot take it. The weather will sometimes deny the use of those kinds we have named to such as are most able to take them: and in this case, any bustling about within doors, whether in the light of business or amusement, will answer the purpose. The adjusting an escritoire, or the new arranging the volumes in a book-case have often produced this good effect; and billiards, or other entertainments which afford means of stirring within the house, answer the same purpose.

To those who are too weak for exercise, even the mildest, and in the best weather, the best relief is a flesh-brush; and its effects are more than can be imagined. We know what we expect from exercise; and in old men, the greatest of its advantages is the assisting circulation. The flesh-brush does this nearly in as great a degree, excepting for the immediate time: but to have the full benefit, it must be constantly and frequently repeated.

Another excellent succedaneum, or substitute, for exercise is washing the body with warm water and rubbing it very well with repeated dry cloaths afterwards. This has many peculiar advantages: the warmth assists perspiration; the washing opens the pores; and the rubbing afterwards is at least equal to the effect of the flesh-brush. The warmth and moisture join also in softening the skin, and rendering it supple; and this is a great point, for it is apt to grow hard and dry with age.

Care must be taken to avoid taking cold after this. The best time for it is evening in a warm bedchamber; and the bed should be ready immediately, that the person may go into it hot.

The hands and feet should have their full share in this washing and rubbing, for the circulation is weakest there, and the pores are most liable to be stopped. The warm bath answers, in some degree, this purpose, and will be spoken of hereafter: but it is rather to be used as a remedy than a preservative; and we are here treating of old men in health.

# CHAPTER VIII

# Of a regulation of the temper. And of the passions

WITHOUT entering into the province of the moralist or preacher, we may say the passions demand great regard in preserving the health of old men. The motion of the blood in circulation is greatly affected and altered by them; and the nerves suffer more. The whole frame is disordered; and I have often seen disease, and sometimes immediate death the consequence of giving full way to them.

Nothing in this world is worth the trouble and distress men bring upon themselves about it, by giving way to immoderate passions. Life is the greatest blessing, and health the next; and these suffer by that fond indulgence.

That the circulation is disordered by passions, we know from the true and certain indication of the pulse. In anger it beats violent and hard; in grief faint and slow; terrors make it irregular; and shame impedes its motions.

These are sure notices of a disordered circulation; and old men cannot bear this even for a time without damage. The strength of youth restores all to its former state when the gust is over: but age is weak, and cannot. Philosophy teaches the governing of our passions; and it is true wisdom. The old man should love himself too well to indulge them. It is not worth his while. Quiet and regularity of life in every respect are his business:

and as he is past the fluttering pleasures of youth, let him place himself above its troubles.

Good humour, and a satisfaction of mind will give the aged many more years, and much happiness in them. Discontent and disturbance wear out nature: but the temper, we advise, preserves her in good condition.

Of all passions let the old man avoid a foolish fondness for women. This never will solicit him, for nature knows her own time, and the appetite decays with the power; but if he solicit that which he cannot enjoy, he will disturb his constitution more than by any other means whatever; and while he is shortening his life; and robbing the poor remainder of the benefits of peace, he will be only making himself the ridicule of those who seem to favour his vain and ineffectual desires.

In passionate people, what we blame as their fault, is often their misfortune. Some, from a tyrannical disposition, have fixed this humour upon themselves by custom, with no other cause: but for each one of these there are a hundred whose fury of temper is owing to a disorder in their body.

We know madness is a disease; and violent passion is a temporary madness. This also arises often from a redundance of humours, and medicines will cure it.

Let the passionate old man consider, that he hurts himself more than anybody else, by his anger; and he will then wish to be cured of its tyranny. Let him examine himself, whether it be a disorder of his mind; and his physician, whether it lie in his body. In the first case, the remedy is philosophy, but in the latter, a few medicines will restore him to temper: to that temper on which his life and happiness depend.

Let the hasty old man cool himself by physic and a low diet: and let him who is melancholy and gloomy banish the everlasting fear of death by warmer foods, cordial medicines, and that best of cordials, wine. These will drive away much more than the apprehension of death, they will put off the reality: for melancholy would have sunk the feeble, long before his time.

Of all states in the mind, a disturb'd hurry of the nerves is most to be avoided. The blood and spirits are disorder'd by this much more than by

exercise, or bodily motion; and they are much longer in coming to themselves again. Exercise ceases absolutely when 'tis over: but the storms of the mind leave a swelling sea, which strength of body alone can calm; and in age this strength is faint.

No disease is more mischievous to weak old persons than a purging: and I have seen this brought on instantly by a fit of passion, or a fright. Medicines have attempted to relieve the patient in vain. That which would have been stop'd, if natural, by a spoonful of chalk julep, or a dose of diascordium, has in this case reduced the person to a skeleton, and sunk him into the grave in spite of all help.

Why should the old man disturb his mind with passion? Or what should he dread? Death is his great terror; and he is very absurd who brings it on by lesser fears.

Joy, tho' only a greater degree of satisfaction, is in a violent or outrageous degree as hurtful as the other passions. It hurries the circulation vehemently and irregularly; it exhausts the spirits; and it has often occasioned sudden death. It is a violence of youth; it belongs to that period of life properly that can bear it, and to that let us leave it. Let the old man be as the Quakers in this point, always cheerful but never merry.

Last let me caution the aged man who would be happy, and would live much longer, to combat with all his power that dangerous enemy covetousness. 'Tis known universally, and we have sacred attestation of it, that too earnest carefulness brings age before its time; and in age it brings death prematurely. The old are in no danger of extravagance; and the care of heaping up for others, when it shortens their own life, is more than any heir can deserve from them.

Ease and good humour are the great ingredients of a happy life, and the principal means of a long one. The whole lesson extends but thus much farther: that the old man love life so well, and value so little all the accidents that belong to it, that he should not give a vain attention to a part which may rob him of the whole.

# CHAPTER IX

## *Of sleep for old men*

INTEMPERANCE has converted day into night, in the course of the gay young world, but this need not influence those in years. Midnight entertainments are no part of the economy of their peaceful lives; therefore they may come nearer to the course of nature.

The quantity of sleep is a material article; and the time not less. The old man has been cautioned against the cold air of evenings; and after a light supper, and an hour or two of social conversation with his family and his neighbours, bed will be his best place.

Sleep was intended to recruit nature, and restore the wasted spirits. This is necessary to all persons, but to the aged most, because they can least bear the waste of them. The passions will disturb all constitutions, but those of old persons most: sleep composes these. Therefore 'tis of excellent use to them: and they may indulge in it longer than the young.

Six hours is as much as a person in the prime of life should sleep: but in age eight or ten, according to the peculiar constitution, will be more proper.

The natural season of sleep is night, and let the old man go to bed in such time that he may pass these hours of rest without breaking in upon the morning. In general the most healthful custom is to go to bed at ten at night and rise at eight in the morning.

If the mind be hurry'd, or from any other cause the person finds he cannot compose himself to rest soon after going to bed, let him still rise at the same time the following morning: and the next evening prepare himself for better sleep. Let him go into a warm bath; and indulge himself with a glass of wine, beyond the ordinary allowance, a little before bedtime. This will take off his watchfulness; and he will sink into the most pleasing slumber.

The contrary practice of lying in bed in the morning, to make up for want of sleep at night,

is in every way extremely wrong. As nothing refreshes like seasonable sleep, so nothing weakens and dejects a person more than long lying in bed in the morning. There is also this farther ill consequence, that the person is never sleepy again at the due time of the evening succeeding; and thus what was at first an accident, becomes by indulgence a custom; the more difficult to be conquer'd and the more hurtful.

He who has observed a temperate diet, and goes to bed at ten o'clock, will naturally wake towards eight: and when he wakes let him get up: he will then be in spirits for the day. If on the contrary he lies dosing, he will get into a weakening sweat: and he will be low spirited during the following day, and waking and watchful at night.

On these little circumstances do the health or sickness, the happiness or uneasiness of old persons depend in a great measure. We do not perceive them, or we overlook them: let us be for the future more careful. There is no pain in the living regularly in old age; and the consequence of it is certain, a longer life, and every day of it more agreeable.

## CHAPTER X

# *Of the particular faults in old men's constitutions*

HITHERTO we have treated of the condition of persons advanced in years who are healthy: and the rules we have laid down are for preserving and continuing that state. He who observes them duly will not fail of success.

We now shall consider the several faults in the constitution at this period of life; and the diseases rising from them. The old man may be so far his own doctor, as to amend the general distemperature of his body, and to prevent those diseases: but if he fall into them, by neglect of these cautions, or in spite of their force, let him then call in the physician. We can advise him how to preserve health when he has it; and how to remedy general disorders so as to prevent more particular ones, if a due regimen may do that: but he is a very ill judge of the human frame, who will pretend to remedy its diseases without knowledge in its structure, and the virtues of remedies; and he would be a bad member of society who gave such advice. It were as easy to teach any other art by writing; and as rational to attempt making a watchmaker, or a shipbuilder, by descriptions of the tools. The whole life of the physician spent in attention and experience hardly qualifies him for the undertaking: how then should a few words give due information?

# CHAPTER XI

## *Of a fullness of blood*

An overfullness of blood naturally brings on a redundance of the other humours: for as they are separated from the blood, they naturally encrease with it in quantity; and the one or the other may, and naturally will, occasion disorders; much more both.

The old man may know he has too much blood in his veins from these plain symptoms: his pulse will be full and strong, and quicker than it should; his complexion ruddy; and his urine high coloured. The veins also will be swelled, and his breathing difficult.

The occasion of all this has been too large feeding, and too little exercise: therefore the plain method to abate the symptoms, and prevent the mischief they threaten, is by more motion, and an abstemious diet.

This is the change to be made: but it must not be sudden. We have observed before, that all hasty alterations are dangerous, but as this is slowly, let it be regularly brought on. As there is in such a case no disease come on as yet from the fullness, there will not any come on during a gradual course of emptying the vessels by this practice. Nature will be relieved thus in a satisfactory manner, whereas she would have been too violently disturbed by a shock.

The first rule is to retrench one third part from the flesh eaten at dinner; of whatever kind that be. We have advised the abstaining from beef and pork: but in this case mutton should be also let alone, or very rarely eaten. The dinner being made solely of the tender and young meats in this reduced quantity, the next care must be, that these are always well and thoroughly done.

Let the person rise an hour before the usual time in the morning, and every day increase the quantity of exercise a little: but with great care not to go out at improper hours to endanger taking cold. In getting rid of one evil, let us not run into another. This fullness is a state in which diseases are most easily brought on, and will be most violent. Colds are very dangerous to people in this condition, and therefore are most carefully to be avoided.

The pulse will shew whether this method reduces the redundance: and if it do not take a visible effect in five days, it will be proper to be blooded. After this the same regimen will compleat the business, and there will be no need for medicines.

If all this fail, the warm bath every other day will probably answer the purpose. In all old men's cases 'tis best to avoid medicines, if it could be done with safety, for they disturb the constitution: and the best guard of these person's health is quietness.

# CHAPTER XII

## Of wasting and decay

WHEN OLD PERSONS fall into this condition, it generally carries them off. But many may be saved by timely care, to whom no remedies will be service after a first neglect. While the stomach is able to digest any thing, there is hope of recovery, but when its power is lost, food and physick are thrown down the throat in vain.

When an old man perceives his flesh wasting, and his strength and spirits failing, let him take good nourishment, and adapt it to the condition of his stomach. If it be too strong, or if he take too much, the digestive faculty, impaired by general weakness, cannot manage it. He will hasten his death by such a conduct.

The rule is to eat only innocent and nourishing things, and these in moderate quantities: chicken, young lamb, and veal boiled down almost to jelly,

are the proper foods for dinner, and of these let him eat less than his appetite demands.

Two hours before dinner, let him take half a pint of chicken broth; and as his stomach strengthens, veal or mutton broth; and the same one hour after his light dinner.

Let the breakfast be a yolk of an egg, beaten up with half a pint of asses milk, and a quarter of an ounce of conserve of roses: and his supper veal broth nearly boiled to a jelly.

Every afternoon let him take half a pint of asses milk alone: and while this is doing, let there be no violent evacuations. A purging would be destructive; and morning sweats are very hurtful. Let him therefore rise early: and to compleat the cure, let him believe these methods will perform it. An easy mind will do more than food or physic.

Quiet, good humour, and complacency of temper will prevent half the diseases of old people; and cure many of the others.

# CHAPTER XIII

## *Against sharp humours*

THE first sign of sharp humours in the bodies of old persons is an uneasiness in the stomach: then comes on a want of appetite, with four belchings, wind, purgings, and defluctions; thirst, and a feverish disposition.

The fault lies originally in the stomach; and generally an irregular diet has been the cause: high sauces, bad wines, and spicy foods. The first step to a cure is to abstain from these; and life depends upon it: for to aggravate those symptoms is to destroy the constitution utterly: incurable fevers, or fatal purgings follow.

The best beginning is by a vomit: and after this the diet must be all of the mild and cooling kind. Every morning let the person take two spoonfuls of syrup of snails made by bruising them with sugar, and hanging them up in a flannel bag till the juice runs out: and at meals, let the drink be a tea made of marshmallow and liquorice-root, with one third part milk, and drank just warm. If skin grow yellow, or the white of the eyes appear of that colour, a dose of rhubarb once in three days will be needful. The best method of taking it is by chewing.

This is as much physick as we would have the old man use in such a case: the rest must be done by a proper regimen. Let him regulate his passions: violent anger will increase this disorder more than the most improper foods. Let him also banish fear. If he thinks himself in danger, he will bring on that danger.

He must never overload his stomach; nor ever suffer it to be empty. Once in two hours he should swallow something. Jellies of hartshorn, truly made, are excellent, but they must be prepared at home: for cheating is so easy, and the true method with hartshorn only is so tedious, that few who make them for sale will do it honestly.

Often this complaint rises from a stoppage of perspiration in some part, particularly in the feet. Then the business is to bring it on again by additional warmth: as by flannel socks and yarn

stockings. This will in many cases alone perform the cure; and in all others, where such a stoppage has been a part of the cause, it will assist the other methods.

The pulse, which was at first too quick, will grow moderate as these cautions take place, and this promises a cure. To compleat it, the patient must go to bed in time, and use moderate exercise in the best hours of the day. He must eat no fat meats, drink little wine, and avoid care and uneasiness of mind.

If he do not sleep well, he must take a small dose of syrup of diacodium every night.

This method will restore him to health, and it must be preserved with due care afterwards, else relapses in this case are frequent. A vomit once in six weeks and a dose of rhubarb every ten days, with a careful diet, will make this a very healthy constitution.

The great care is taking the defect in time; for new disorders are easily conquered, but established ones are too obstinate for such constitutions.

# CHAPTER XIV

# Of pain and inflammations

IT IS proper to treat of these together, because they generally come together. We need not tell the old man where he is in pain: but he must examine carefully whether there be inflammation with it.

This he will know by his pulse beating hard and quick, and by high coloured urine: his flesh also will be hotter than usual. When pains come on without these symptoms, warmth in the part, and patience are the remedies. They must be considered as the lot of age, and borne accordingly: but when these symptoms join with them they threaten dangerous consequences.

The first step is bleeding: and this with abstinence from all hot foods often performs the cure.

If there be no relief, the next day but one, a vomit will be proper. If the body be costive, it

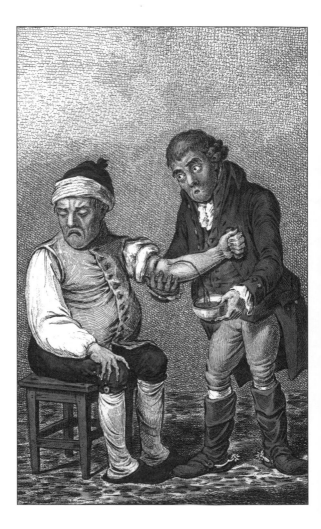

inflames all the symptoms: and if purges be given, they increase the violent motion of the blood, and therefore do more hurt than service. Cooling and oily glysters are the proper method; and they should be repeated every morning.

The diet must be light and cool. All solid foods should be omitted for the first four or five days, and in their place asses milk should be taken: and chicken broth and jellies must be the nourishment during this period.

After this, as the disorder abates, the strength must be considered; and by degrees the usual diet such as is here recommended for healthy old men may be introduced. But this must be done gradually, and with great caution; otherwise, sudden change, from low to richer diet, will certainly bring on the complaint again; and worse inflammation.

# CHAPTER XV

## *Of fluxes*

AGED PEOPLE bear a too costive habit much
better than they do fluxes or purgings: for they
are easily weakened; and nothing does it more
than these.

The great rule in old men's disorders is to take them in time. This will be cured by proper diet when it is regarded early: otherwise medicines must be called in, and perhaps they will be ineffectual.

The quantity of solid food should be abated, but it should not be left off wholly. The drink should be made of burnt hartshorn and comfry root, two ounces of each boiled in two quarts of water to three pints, the liquor poured clear off, and drank warm with a little red wine.

Rice-milk, with some cinnamon boiled in it, is excellent for breakfast; and rice-pudding for supper; two hours before bedtime. Sea-biscuit should be eaten instead of bread, and the patient must use more than ordinary exercise, to promote perspiration.

# CHAPTER XVI

## *Of the gravel & stone*

OLD PERSONS are very subject to obstructions in the urinary passages; and the various degrees of the gravel and stone follow. These are disorders difficult of cure, but they are easily prevented in most constitutions.

Let those who are subject to slight complaints of this kind avoid wine, and supply its place by beer of a due strength.

Let the diet be cooling: and in regard to exercise, the rule is moderation. Violent motion, or rest for a long time together, are equally wrong. Let the patient walk every day in the proper hours; and when the weather does not permit that, let him use the same exercise in his chamber.

When fits come on, let him take manna and oil: this is an easy and effectual medicine. Two ounces of manna should be dissolved in half a pint of water, and six spoonfuls of sallad oil added to it. A spoonful of this taken every half hour will stay upon the stomach, assuage pain, stop the vomitings which often attend this complaint; and at the same time procure stools: and while it eases the cholick pains will give passage to the stone.

This is the course in the violence of a fit. When it is perceived coming on, an infusion of burdock root slic'd, is the best remedy. Two ounces of the fresh root and a quart of boiling water poured on it makes this infusion. The liquor is to be strained off as soon as cold: and half a pint, a little warmed again, with a quarter of a pint of milk, and sweetened with honey, is to be taken every four hours.

This is the medicine lately published for the gout; and which many are now taking for that disease with great success. The gout and gravel are nearly ally'd, and it is not strange the same remedy is so effectual also in this case. The wonder is, that a plant of great virtue, and so common, has been so long neglected by the practitioners of physick.

Of the gout it would be vain to treat here. 'Tis a peculiar subject, and requires a larger compass than any single article can be allowed in this work.

# CHAPTER XVII

# *Of weakness*

OLD MEN must expect a decay of strength: and it would be as idle to call it a disease, as vain to think of remedies. But, besides this which is natural and necessary, weakness is sometimes accidental, and it may thus be remedied.

Great evacuations, intense study, violent passions, or a too low diet will sometimes bring it on before the natural time, and a proper care and regimen may remove it.

A lowness of the pulse, feebleness of the limbs, a paleness of the face, waste of flesh, and low spirits are the symptoms by which this is known; and the remedies are cordial medicines, and a somewhat richer diet.

The medicine I have found most effectual is this: a quarter of an ounce of saffron, a dram of cinnamon, and an ounce of confection alkermes in a quart of white wine. When this has stood two days it should be poured off; and half a wine glass of it drank once a day.

Rest of mind and body are also in this case great articles toward the cure. Let not the patient think he is in danger: let him venture to eat somewhat richer meats, but in a moderate quantity, and indulge in one extraordinary glass of wine at every meal.

Let him rise early; but not go out till the air is well warmed by the sun, and the dews are

dispersed. If he reside in London at the time, let him immediately go into the country: if he be too loose in his bowels let him check it moderately by the means we have directed; and let his malt liquor be strong of the hop.

Between breakfast and dinner let him every day take a yolk of a new laid egg beat up in a glass of strong white wine. The company of agreeable friends will be the best medicine in an evening; and good broth his fittest supper.

# CHAPTER XVIII

## Of the asthma

THIS IS A COMMON COMPLAINT with aged persons; and there is none more troublesome. 'Tis difficult of cure, but relief is easy: and it will depend as much on the air as all other considerations together. The great care in this respect is that the air of the place be neither thick nor damp.

The smoak of London is very bad; and the ill smells from many of the trades carried on there is as hurtful. No person subject to an asthma should live near tanners in the country, nor tallow chandlers, or the like offensive trades in London.

Exercise at proper times is vastly beneficial in this case. Walking or riding before dinner and supper are particularly proper. Frequent washing the feet in warm water, with good rubbing with dry cloaths afterwards, is also highly serviceable.

All cold and vicious foods must be avoided. The stomach must not be suffered to be empty, nor must it be loaded. The food should be of the richest kind that is proper for persons advanced in years; and to assist digestion two or three dishes of good tea, made carefully and taken with little sugar and without milk, should be drank constantly, two hours and a half after dinner.

Vegetables should be avoided; and one great caution should be not to drink too much of any liquor whatsoever.

Bleeding is usually necessary; and the condition of the blood will shew whether it should be in larger or smaller quantity; and whether or not it will require to be soon repeated.

If the blood be fizey these repeated bleedings will be necessary; and the same condition of it shews the body can spare these quantities. It shews also, that without these bleedings medicines can take no effect.

After this the greatest preservative against sharp or repeated fits is the famous gum ammoniacum. A quarter of an ounce of this being dissolved in half a pint of water, two spoonfuls should be taken, according to the symptoms, each night, or every second or third night.

This method will prevent many fits; and abate the severity of those which cannot be put off. Thus the old man, even against the fury of this worst disturbance of his life, and all the rest, will live happy: and he ought to value that happiness the more because he will owe it to his own discretion.